of the greatest photographs in
Liverpool Football Club's history.

It is not a definitive A to Z of every player who
has played for the club. It is filled with the heroes.
The legends. The forgotten men. The action.
The drama. The tears. The laughter. The goals.
The glory. The unexpected.

Like the bedroom of the boy who passi
decorates his walls with pictures of his
This is a shrine to by far the greatest
– and images – the world has ever see

LIVERPOOL
FOOTBALL CLUB

A to Z
GREATEST PICTURES
THE OFFICIAL COLLECTION

Published in Great Britain in 2010 by:
Trinity Mirror Sport Media,
PO Box 48, Old Hall Street,
Liverpool L69 3EB
Hardback version orgininally printed in 2006

Executive Editor: KEN ROGERS
Senior Editor: STEVE HANRAHAN
Senior Art Editor: RICK COOKE
Senior Production Editor: PAUL DOVE
Senior Sub Editor: ROY GILFOYLE
Sub Editor: ADAM OLDFIELD
Writers: CHRIS McLOUGHLIN, JOHN HYNES, ALAN JEWELL,
SIMON HUGHES, WILLIAM HUGHES, JAMES CLEARY
Designers: LISAMARIE CRITCHLEY, LEE ASHUN, GLEN HIND, COLIN SUMPTER,
BARRY PARKER, ALISON GILLILAND, JAMES KENYON, JAMIE DUNMORE
Sales and Marketing Manager: ELIZABETH MORGAN

ISBN 9781906802288

Photographs: Liverpool Daily Post and Echo. Trinity Mirror. Liverpool Football Club. Empics. Additional images: David Rawcliffe (p13)

Printed by Broad Link Enterprise Ltd

LIVERPOOL
FOOTBALL CLUB

A to Z
GREATEST PICTURES
THE OFFICIAL COLLECTION

One of the most famous images in the world hangs on the wall of the Louvre Museum. Its subject's enigmatic smile captivates millions, but it is the disbelieving grin on Alan Kennedy's face when he grabbed the winner against Real Madrid in the 1981 European Cup final that stirs the soul of Liverpudlians.

Our own Paris masterpiece.

Rome conjures up eternal images of the elation of Emlyn as he lifts the trophy for the first time. The sight of Shankly on the steps of St George's Hall greeting the red and white masses with his arms raised wide like the Messiah. Kenny dinking the ball over the Bruges keeper, Supersub jumping for joy against St Etienne, Jerzy doing the Brucie wobble in Istanbul and Stevie G beating his chest in front of his beloved Kop after another wonder strike.

Treasured images buried deep in Reds fans' minds and hearts.

ABOVE: Kopites thought they were going to cheer on the 'Pool in the first leg of the UEFA Cup final against Borussia Moenchengladbach in May 1973, but all they got to see was a lake. A downpour just before kick-off quickly turned into a torrential storm and the match was abandoned after 27 minutes. The Reds won 3-0 the next night, and hung on to clinch the trophy despite a 2-0 defeat in Germany

Abandoned matches

FROM TOP: Officials can barely see each other as they decide the Reds' League Cup clash with Arsenal in December 2006 must be called off

Bill Shankly isn't a happy man as he trudges off the waterlogged White Hart Lane pitch with his Spurs counterpart Bill Nicholson in February 1974

It's off again. Ronnie Moran and his team-mates can't believe the state of the Worcester pitch three days after the previous postponement. The tie was jinxed. The Reds eventually crashed 2-1 to the underdogs, one of our worst ever FA Cup defeats

A'Court, Alan

ABOVE: The Swansea goalkeeper's right fist wasn't strong enough to repel this A'Court shot that found its way into the top corner of the net via the inside of the upright

LEFT: You put your right leg in. A'Court was subject to a few crude challenges in his 381-game Liverpool career but few so crude as this one from a game with Northampton Town in the FA Cup in 1958

ABOVE: Now we see why A'Court managed such a respectable goals total, 63 in 300-plus appearances - goal-poaching was his speciality! Despite loitering with intent he didn't get his name on the scoresheet as Liverpool hammered Bury 4-1 at Anfield

RIGHT: Even at a stretch A'Court couldn't put this effort against Sheffield Wednesday into the net but it's the Kemlyn Road stand - or more precisely the lack of one - in the background, as it underwent construction work, that really catches the eye in this picture from April 1963

Aldridge, John

The adulation in the young Liverpool fans' faces says it all as Aldo celebrates his first goal in the opening game of the 1988/89 season away to Charlton. The striker went on to complete a hat-trick in a 3-0 win

Aldridge, John

TOP: No sign of pre-match nerves. In fact Aldo was feeling "sound as a pound" as he prepared for his Anfield debut against Southampton in February, 1987. He didn't disappoint, scoring past England keeper Peter Shilton with a flying header

ABOVE: John Aldridge stretches to get on the end of a brilliant John Barnes cross to volley home the BBC goal of the season against Nottingham Forest at Hillsborough in the semi-final of the 1988 FA Cup. He also scored a penalty to make it 2-0 to the Reds

Alonso, Xabi

Xabi's team-mates are furious as he attempts an audacious shot on goal in injury time from well inside his own half with the Luton keeper stranded but the classy midfielder hits the target to make it 5-3 in one of the greatest comebacks in FA Cup history in January 2006. Liverpool were 3-1 down in the second half

Arrowsmith, Alf

Bill Shankly described Alf Arrowsmith as 'born to score goals' and he was only prevented from adding another to his 24-strike Reds total by an acrobatic save from the Swansea goalkeeper. Arrowsmith averaged a goal every other game in a Liverpool career cut short by injury

Attack, attack, attack!

"You made a mess of the first match - now show what you can do!" That was the message from Bob Paisley to his players after Liverpool had laboured to a 1-1 draw with Finnish minnows Oulu Palloseura in the opening game of the glorious 1980-1981 European Cup campaign. The same team was named and they responded emphatically. David Fairclough (pictured right) scored twice as the Reds made it 10-1 on the night. Amazingly, had it not been for the Finnish part-timers' offside trap - the Liverpool players were caught offside 25 times that night - the Reds might have shattered the European goalscoring record

Would you believe it? On the night Liverpool smashed ten goals past the helpless Finns, Kenny Dalglish just couldn't score . . . but the King saw the funny side

Barnes, John

TOP: Steve McMahon and Gary Ablett wait for John Barnes to come back down to earth after he put Liverpool ahead in an FA Cup fourth round tie at Villa Park in 1988. The massed ranks of the old Holte End can be seen in the background

LEFT: Another Barnes special has the beating of Hans Segers in September 1990. The tiny crowd overlooked by a toilet. It could only be Plough Lane

RIGHT: Barnes congratulates Peter Beardsley after the latter has put Liverpool 3-0 up against Everton at Goodison in September 1990. The final score was 3-2

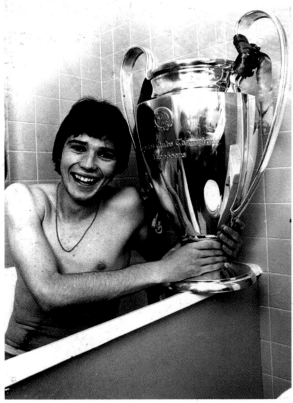

Bath time

TOP: Soaking it up. The Liverpool squad in 1950 after beating Everton in the FA Cup semi-final at Maine Road. The goalscorers in that game, Bob Paisley and Billy Liddell, are at the back of the bath on the left

ABOVE: Soaper star Emlyn flanked by Brian Hall and Tommy Smith. Steve Heighway is in the foreground

LEFT: Alan Hansen and a European Cup-shaped bath toy after Liverpool beat Bruges at Wembley in 1978

Beardsley, Peter

TOP: Beardsley has just scored his second of a hat-trick against Manchester United in September 1990. The eyes of Beardsley, Neil Webb and Les Sealey appear to be directed at a linesman. The flag stayed down

RIGHT: "Nice one Peter, lad." A young boy congratulates Beardsley after Liverpool beat Everton 1-0 in an FA Cup fifth round tie at Goodison Park in February 1988

BELOW: Derek Mountfield and Paul McGrath of Aston Villa are powerless to prevent Beardsley scoring at Anfield in September 1990

Benitez, Rafael

LEFT: Rafa reminds his squad how many European Cups the club has won as they went in search of another against Chelsea in the 2009 Champions League quarter-finals

MIDDLE: One of the unforeseen side-effects of the Icelandic volanic ash cloud in 2010 that grounded hundreds of flights was Rafa having to share a train buffet car with a clutch of journalists as he held an impromptu press conference on the way to play Atletico Madrid in the Europa League semi-final first leg

BOTTOM: Rafa can't hide his delight as he gets his hands on the European Cup in his first season in charge of the Reds, making it a famous five for the most successful club in British history

Boersma, Phil

A run without reward. Phil Boersma has to
turn around after Derby goalkeeper Colin
Boulton gathers at the Baseball Ground in
September 1973

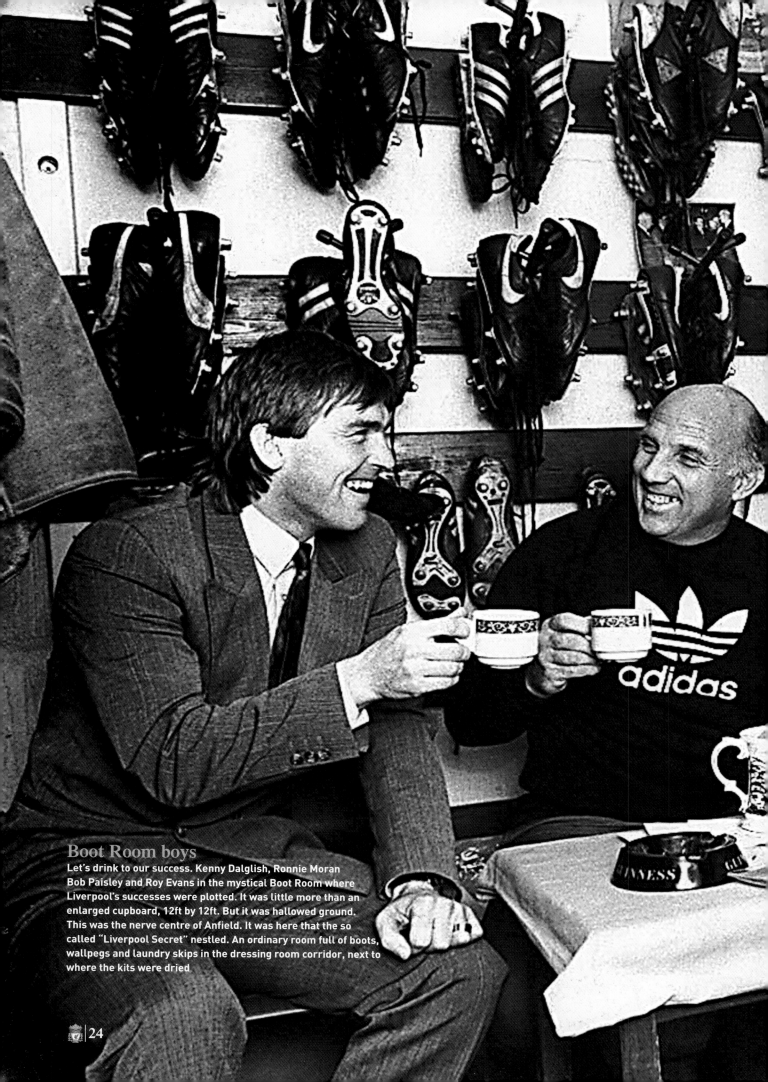

Boot Room boys

Let's drink to our success. Kenny Dalglish, Ronnie Moran
Bob Paisley and Roy Evans in the mystical Boot Room where
Liverpool's successes were plotted. It was little more than an
enlarged cupboard, 12ft by 12ft. But it was hallowed ground.
This was the nerve centre of Anfield. It was here that the so
called "Liverpool Secret" nestled. An ordinary room full of boots,
wallpegs and laundry skips in the dressing room corridor, next to
where the kits were dried

Byrne, Gerry

TOP: The referee has his whistle to his lips and is blowing for a foul, presumably a push in the back on fearless full-back Gerry Byrne. The tough defender famously played on in the 1965 FA Cup final with a broken collar bone

RIGHT: No messin' about. Byrne sends the ball skywards and Geoff Strong, later to sign for Liverpool, is the Arsenal player flinching in this Highbury match from March 1963. Tommy Lawrence and Ronnie Moran stand behind Byrne

BOTTOM: Gerry Byrne and Ron Yeats go to ground to block Luton's path in a Second Division game from November 1961

Callaghan, Ian

'Super Cally' arrived in 1960 and took the place of his hero Billy Liddell. Callaghan was applauded off the pitch by his team-mates on his debut. Here he is applauded onto it by the fans. The Liverpool-born teenager was a rampaging right winger for a decade, but in 1971 he suffered knee damage and when he re-gained his place it was in the centre of midfield

TOP LEFT: Callaghan heads the first of his two goals in this 3-2 win at Craven Cottage past helpless Fulham goalkeeper Tony Macedo as the Cottagers' Bobby 'Killer' Keetch looks on in March 1965

MIDDLE: Ian Callaghan is pictured celebrating a remarkable 800 appearances for Liverpool against Derby in February, 1977. The player, who was never sent off in nearly two full decades, and was booked only once, added another 57 appearances to that total before leaving Anfield for Swansea the following year

BOTTOM: Cally places the ball beyond Peter Shilton's reach to complete a goal rush that saw Liverpool 4-0 up against Leicester after just 12 minutes in September 1968

Canteen

This is the 'chillout zone' at the back of the
Anfield canteen in the Seventies. It looks a bit
like an airport lounge but it was somewhere
the first-teamers enjoyed relaxing and having
a cup of tea

Camara, Titi

An emotional Titi Camara sheds a tear and says
a prayer for his father who had sadly passed
away just hours before the Guinea striker scored
in front of the Anfield Road fans in this 1-0 win over West Ham
in October '99

Carragher, Jamie

This Bootle schoolboy epitomises the Liverpool spirit today as our longest serving player. Jamie Carragher, or 'Carra' as his team-mates call him, gives everything when he pulls on the famous red shirt. The no-nonsense defender has filled every position in the back four since scoring on his debut against Aston Villa in 1997. Here he is in front of the famous 'This Is Anfield' sign and getting stuck in for Bootle boys (below)

BOTTOM RIGHT: Carra goes on to prove he would do anything for the Liverpool cause by carrying on with a head wound at White Hart Lane on the opening day of the 2009/10 season

Carragher, Jamie
One of us. Carra celebrates with the fans
in Istanbul after our fifth European Cup
triumph in 2005

Case, Jimmy

It's no wonder the Kop christened him the Bionic Boot. Case was one of the hardest hitters of a ball that Anfield has ever witnessed. He was the Stevie G of the Seventies. The fierce tackling midfielder who joined Liverpool as an amateur from South Liverpool in 1972. Here he is (left) enjoying a 'Case' of Moet champagne after Liverpool's FA Cup semi-final replay victory over Everton at Maine Road. Case scored late on as the Reds won 3-0

TOP RIGHT: Jimmy Case powers a free-kick through the Norwich wall to seal a 4-1 win at Carrow Road

MIDDLE: With best mate Ray Kennedy, preparing to rip through the Forest. Nottingham, that is, in the League Cup final at Wembley in March 1978. The game finished 0-0, however, and the Reds eventually lost the replay 1-0

BOTTOM: Many fans remember him chesting the ball down and spectacularly volleying it into the Manchester United net in the 1977 FA Cup final. That goal alone deserved to win the trophy, but here he is trying an overhead kick in the same game

Clemence, Ray

RIGHT: Jumping for joy. Clem celebrates another Liverpool goal on a quiet day at the office

TOP: The Liverpool and England keeper dives to save a close-range header from Doncaster striker O'Callaghan to ensure the Reds progress 2-0 through this FA Cup third round replay at Belle Vue in January 1974

ABOVE: Clemence kept another clean sheet in the next round, but only just, as this shot rebounds back off a post in another replay, this time up at Carlisle

LEFT: Clemence leads the way through a group of female fans waiting to catch a glimpse of the team

Dalglish, Kenny

The King is dead. Long live the King.
When Kevin Keegan left in 1977, Kopites
feared the end of a dynasty - until the majestic
Kenny Dalglish pulled on the number seven
shirt in front of his loyal subjects.
Kenny is pictured above relaxing on the team
bus on the way to Highbury for a league match
in the 1983-84 season. Liverpool beat Arsenal
2-0 that day with Dalglish scoring

LEFT: Two goals in a 5-0 win over Danish side
BK Odense and Dalglish celebrates breaking
Denis Law's British scoring record in the
European Cup in September 1983

RIGHT: Bubble King Kenny takes on Everton's
Bob Latchford ahead of a derby game

Dalglish, Kenny

TOP: A typically audacious attempt at a lob from Kenny against Derby

MIDDLE: He's back. Kenny Dalglish returned to Anfield as Academy and Club Ambassador in the summer of 2009 and wowed the youngsters in Thailand during the club's pre-season tour with a training session at the Chulalong stadium

BOTTOM: Sheer determination as Dalglish manages to keep the ball in play during the 1982 League Cup final victory over Spurs at Wembley

FAR RIGHT (left to right): One for the family album as King Kenny brings daughter Kelly along for the ride on the homecoming parade with the 1987-88 League trophy

Not just D for Dalglish, but D for Double. After scoring the goal that clinched the league title in Roy of the Rovers fashion at Stamford Bridge, King Kenny lifts the FA Cup on May 10, 1986, as Liverpool's first ever player-manager

It's not a dream Kenny! It can't be bad waking up in the morning to find this beauty lying next to you . . .

If you look under D in the dictionary for the word 'dink' it reads: "Matchwinning chip-shot invented by Kenny Dalglish in the 1978 European Cup final at Wembley against Bruges" – as seen here in all its glory

Derby games

There's nothing quite like the passion of the Merseyside derby . . .

Dogs on the pitch

Tommy Lawrence, the 'Flying Pig', has a run-in with a fleeing dog, while Bob Paisley takes a cheeky mongrel for a walk off the Anfield pitch

Dressing room

BELOW: A rare picture in the inner sanctum of the
Liverpool dressing room with Bill Shankly giving one
of his legendary team talks
TOP LEFT: A scene from the dressing room in 1950
ABOVE: Heighway sneaks a peek while Cally and
Bobby Graham catch up with the news

Dudek, Jerzy

TOP: Take five. The moment history is made as Jerzy Dudek saves the penalty from Andriy Shevchenko to give Liverpool a 3-2 shoot-out victory after the sensational comeback against Italian giants AC Milan **RIGHT (and below):** The race is on and Jamie Carragher is one of the first on the scene to congratulate the hero of the hour

European Cup

A smile as wide as the Mersey
as Emlyn Hughes lifts the
European Cup for the first time
in Rome, 1977

ABOVE: A mixture of nerves, focus, and sheer amazement as Liverpool's gladiators take in
the sea of red and white as they prepare to do battle in Rome's Olympic stadium in 1977

European Cup: 1977

BELOW: Show us your medals. Goal hero Tommy Smith and Ian Callaghan after the 3-1 victory over Borussia Moenchengladbach

BOTTOM: The start of the love affair. Phil Neal and Jimmy Case enjoy a passionate clinch with the European Cup

European Cup: 1978

Heading home with an extra passenger. David Fairclough, Sammy Lee, Terry McDermott and Richard Money on a special train back to Lime Street after beating Bruges 1-0 at Wembley

European Cup: 1981

A toast to Barney. Cup-lifting skipper Phil Thompson has a pint with match-winning hero Alan Kennedy after the 1981 triumph over Real Madrid in Paris. The European Cup obviously got a taste for it, and would later be spotted back at Kirkby on an impromptu session in Thommo's local pub, 'The Falcon'

ABOVE: Even some of his own team-mates were looking away, but the only mistake Alan Kennedy would make was his choice of celebration after clinching the European Cup once again for the Reds against Roma in their own backyard in '84

BELOW: Phil Neal scores against Roma

European Cup: 1984

ABOVE: Boss Joe Fagan relaxes the following morning by the hotel pool with the European Cup

European Cup: 2005

If you've ever wondered what it must feel like to win the European Cup, just take a look at the faces of the Liverpool players in Istanbul at the moment of realisation a split-second after Jerzy Dudek's match-winning penalty shoot-out save

Evans, Alun

Britain's first £100,000 teenager captured spectacularly in action against Hungarians, Ferencvaros, in the Fairs Cup in 1970. He grabbed a hat-trick against Bayern Munich in the quarter-finals

Evans, Roy

We're used to seeing images of Evans, the manager. Here is Evans the player, with Doug Livermore and Ray Clemence after being told they were in the squad for an Anfield derby in 1970

Exits (emotional)

Three men who shared a common bond. Fighting back the tears as they prepared for the unthinkable . . . the leaving of Liverpool. Shankly looked as numb as the fans at his resignation in 1974, as did Dalglish in 1991. And Aldo, well, he would have stayed if he'd had the choice

FA Cup

New heights. Skipper Ron Yeats and his team-mates celebrate lifting the FA Cup for the first time in 1965 after a 2-1 win over Leeds in extra-time. The FA Cup wasn't always about the magic. Although we've enjoyed six more final victories since 1965, the picture (bottom left) shows Bill Shankly rallying his troops in extra-time for the '71 final against eventual victors Arsenal. It demonstrates what it means to the players, and how those sunny days on the Wembley turf always had a way of sapping the energy from the legs. It was joy all round in 1974, however, as Kevin Keegan and the boys (left) celebrate the beautiful 3-0 demolition of Newcastle. The final in 2006 (top left) has been referred to as the Steven Gerrard final after his heroics against West Ham while Michael Owen was equally responsible for victory in the 2001 final after his dramatic late double rescued the Reds from the clutches of Arsenal

Fagan, Joe

ABOVE: How do you follow Bob Paisley as manager of Liverpool? Easy, become the first-ever manager to win a major treble. That's exactly what Joe Fagan did in his first season in charge in 1983-84. After steering the Reds to a European Cup final again in his second season, the disaster that unfolded before his eyes in Heysel was too much, and he walked away from the club and the game he loved. Here he is saluting the fans on the Kop who don't want the party to end after Liverpool's last home game of the treble-winning season

RIGHT: Fagan steps out with Everton boss Howard Kendall for the 1984 Milk Cup final

LEFT: 'Smokin' Joe Fagan deep in thought in the Liverpool dugout in 1977, while (far right) Fagan and the rest of the bench show no emotion after another Liverpool goal

Fairclough, David

LEFT: Fairclough gets down to business with some press-ups at Melwood

BELOW: It's almost impossible to mention David Fairclough without using the words 'Supersub' or St Etienne in the same sentence. Here he is famously celebrating one of Anfield's greatest European nights after coming from the bench to score the crucial late goal against the classy French outfit to book Liverpool's place in the 1977 European Cup semi-final

Famous Grounds Conquered

The Rafa Benitez era was littered with great results in some of the most impressive cathedrals of world football. Fernando Torres scored the winner as the Reds beat Inter Milan 1-0 at the San Siro in 2008 (top). Craig Bellamy (above right) showed his quali-tee with this golf celebration after a goal in a 2-1 win at the Nou Camp in 2007. Yossi Benayoun got the only goal (right) as the Reds beat Real Madrid at the Bernabeu in 2009

First class Reds

LEFT: First stop London. Next stop Rome. Phil Neal, Terry McDermott and Emlyn Hughes leave Lime Street for the 1977 FA Cup final against Manchester United. The Wembley tears would turn to tears of joy by the time the lads got back from Italy

ABOVE: Jamie Carragher talks and walks at a Paris train station en route to Madrid to play Atletico in 2010

Fowler, Robbie

Could easily have come under 'G' for 'God' or 'Goals'. Fowler was to the Nineties what Rush was to the Eighties and Hunt the Sixties - goalscorer supreme. Here he is (above) as a youngster with Liverpool schoolboys

TOP RIGHT: Fowler is mobbed by his team-mates in front of the Kop after scoring a superb free-kick against Manchester United at Anfield in December 1995. Fowler went on to make it 2-0 in the second half

LEFT: Back of the net, but this time it's Fowler and the ball

RIGHT: Tongue out in typical impish style, celebrating a last minute equaliser against Nottingham Forest in 1995

Garcia, Luis

The little genius has scored some important goals for Liverpool, none more so than the controversial 'did-it or didn't it' (yes, it did) cross the line winner against Chelsea in the Champions League semi-final second leg in May 2005. The tricky Spaniard is pictured keeping his eye on the ball in our main image

TOP LEFT: It's not just with his feet that Garcia is gifted. These celebratory leaps followed a fantastic headed goal in the 3-0 Champions League win over Anderlecht in November 2005 and a crucial goal in the 2006 FA Cup semi-final win against Chelsea at Old Trafford

BOTTOM LEFT: Ju beauty. Garcia scores a stunning left-footed half-volley from 30 yards out. It dipped over the stranded Gianluigi Buffon to give Liverpool a sensational 2-0 lead against the mighty Juventus in the first leg of the quarter-final of the Champions League in April 2005. The game finished 2-1 and the Reds earned an impressive 0-0 draw in Turin to ensure progress

Gerrard, Steven

Bill Shankly once said: "Fire in your belly comes from pride and passion in wearing the red shirt." If ever a modern day Liverpool player epitomises Shankly's words, it is Steven Gerrard when he crosses that white line to play for the club he loves. Ever since he wore the Liver Bird upon his chest for the first time as an 18-year-old, Stevie G has displayed determination, drive, passion and commitment to the Liverpool cause. Add to that a huge helping of talent and ability and you've got some player. As Alan Hansen once put it, he's a 'Souness with pace'. Says it all

Gerrard, Steven

LEFT: With his team 3-0 down against AC Milan in the 2005 Champions League final in Istanbul, the skipper grabbed the game by the scruff of the neck and this towering header sparked the most amazing six-minute comeback of all-time

ABOVE: Another penalty shoot-out, another victory, and Stevie gets to lift the 2006 FA Cup

BELOW: A proud moment as he leads the boys out in Istanbul

RIGHT: It doesn't get any better. Following in the footsteps of Emlyn Hughes, Phil Thompson and Graeme Souness to lift the European Cup for the fifth time

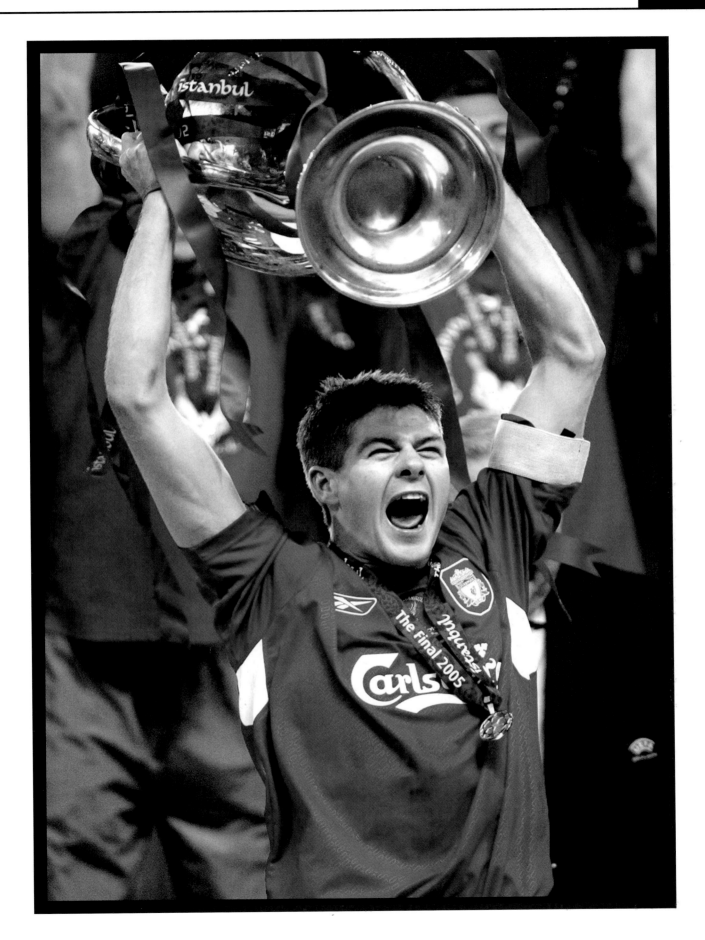

Gerrard, Steven

ABOVE: A giant leap by a giant of Liverpool Football Club, celebrating a goal at Birmingham in 2010

LEFT: One thing Steven Gerrard can never be accused of is not putting his body on the line for the Redmen. He doesn't shirk tackles, he doesn't give up on lost causes. Robbie Savage is feeling the full force of a Gerrard challenge in this picture

RIGHT: How's that for technique! Stevie displays his power, with his head down and both feet off the ground after striking through the ball

BOTTOM LEFT: Stevie silences the Leeds fans at Anfield with Liverpool's third goal in a 3-1 win in March 2003

BOTTOM RIGHT: Can you hear the Blues fans sing, no-oh, no-oh! Steven Gerrard races away after scoring the equaliser against Everton at Goodison in September 2001. A Michael Owen penalty and John Arne Riise strike made it 3-1

Grobbelaar, Bruce

The 'Clown Prince' of football marks the 1983 League Cup final win against Manchester United by walking around Wembley on his hands (top left) and he's at it again (left) balancing an umbrella on his nose after beating Sunderland in the 1992 FA Cup final

FAR LEFT: Bruce Grobbelaar had plenty of time on his hands to knock back the coins that are aimed his way in this 5-0 thumping of Everton at Goodison Park in November 1982. In the same game, Graeme Sharp bears down on goal as Brucie returns to his goalkeeping duties to mop up a rare attack

ABOVE: The evergreen number one proves he has still got it nine years later pulling off one of his trademark 'Hollywood' saves during a 3-1 win over the Blues at Anfield

Hall, Brian

BELOW: A spectacular winning goal from Brian Hall gives Phil Parkes no chance at Molineux in March 1974

RIGHT: As the sign says... Liverpool are on their way to the 1974 FA Cup final as Hall celebrates scoring the opener past Peter Shilton in the semi-final replay victory over Leicester in 1974

Hamann, Dietmar

Liverpool's German destroyer spent seven years breaking up opponents' attacks while at Anfield and here he's at it again, facing up to Wigan's Jimmy Bullard

Hansen, Alan

RIGHT: Thanks for your patients. Hansen gets looked after during a spell on the sidelines

BELOW: Jocky wins a header during his Liverpool league debut in September 1977

MIDDLE: On the biggest stage of all. Hansen keeps the mighty Real Madrid at bay, paving the way for Alan Kennedy's famous winner in the Parc Des Princes in 1981, our third European Cup triumph

BOTTOM: Hansen slides home a late winner against AZ67 Alkmaar in the European Cup second round in October 1981

FAR RIGHT: Sweet taste of success. Celebrating the 1981 League Cup victory against West Ham in which Hansen scored in the Villa Park replay

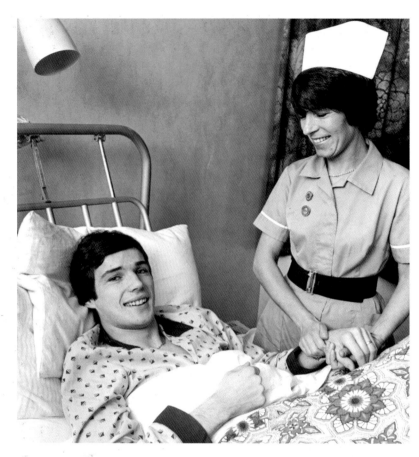

Hateley, Tony

Hateley is horrified
as he misses a sitter with
Gordon Banks, always
popular with the Kop,
stranded in October 1967

Heighway, Steve
Being helped off the pitch by Ronnie
Moran in 1976, as the Kop looks on

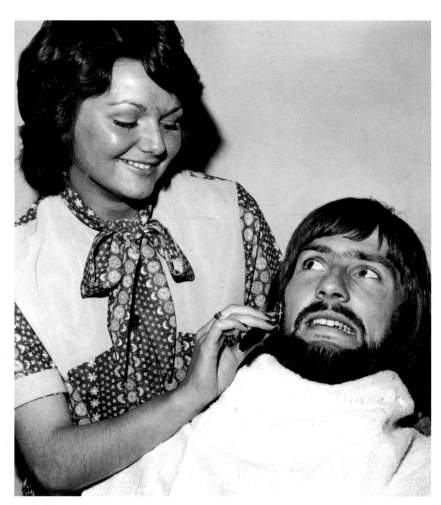

Heighway, Steve

RIGHT: A close shave. The beard came off two days before an FA Cup final date with Newcastle in 1974. It proved to be a wise move – Heighway and the Reds were a cut above the Geordies

BELOW: A model pro. It looks like a scene from the movie Saturday Night Fever as Heighway and Phil Thompson don the white suits for a modelling assignment in June 1978

Hillsborough disaster

BOTTOM: Flowers and tributes cover the Anfield pitch in the immediate aftermath of the Hillsborough disaster in 1989

BELOW: A packed Anfield remembers the 96 victims 20 years on

LEFT: One of the candles lit in 2010 to remember the disaster's victims

Homecomings

LEFT: If this is the turnout when we lose (Arsenal FA Cup final, 1971) what will it be like when we win? That question was answered on many glorious occasions but the sea of red and white that engulfed the city to welcome home the heroes of Istanbul in 2005 takes some beating

Homecomings

ABOVE: Not a bad present to bring home for the fans in your first season in charge. Rafael Benitez with the 2005 European Cup

BELOW: Magnums of champagne and a 'Magnum' (Tom Selleck) look-a-like as Graeme Souness and his team-mates show off the 1984 European Cup. Ronnie Whelan appears well-refreshed, while keen photographer Craig Johnston records the day for posterity

Houllier, Gerard

RIGHT: You wait ages for a trophy and then three come along at once. A triumphant Gerard Houllier and his players return from Dortmund with the UEFA Cup to add to the FA Cup and League Cup collection of 2000-01

BELOW: An emotional moment for the boss and the fans as he returns for his first game back in charge against Roma in 2002 after life-saving heart surgery

Hughes, Emlyn

ABOVE: Two icons of Merseyside football who never gave less than their best. Emlyn consoles Alan Ball after Liverpool have beaten Everton in the 1971 FA Cup semi-final. He appears about to fall into the embrace of a fan

RIGHT: Emlyn gives the Reds plenty to shout about at Goodison, scoring the first of his double in a 2-0 win over our derby rivals in March 1973

TOP RIGHT: Unable to contain his delight after the second of his two goals in that 1973 Goodison derby

Hughes, Emlyn

ABOVE: Work rest and play. Emlyn on a sleeper train back from a game in the capital

RIGHT: Prior to the 1974 FA Cup final, Emlyn flirting with Princess Anne, a routine he would later repeat as team captain on 'A Question of Sport'

BELOW: Emlyn helps to launch a skateboard park at Southport Pleasure Beach and takes part in an archery contest with Bob Latchford (right) to promote Father's Day in 1978

From lifting the European Cup to lifting sheds. It's amazing in this day and age to look back at how the conqueror of Rome (above) and Football Writers' Player of the Year spent the summer months of 1977. Here he is pitching in at his dad's Tarmacadam-laying business back in his home town of Barrow in Furness

Hughes, Emlyn

ABOVE: Despair for West Ham's Bobby Moore as Hunt wheels away in delight after scoring in an FA Cup quarter-final in March 1963

LEFT: Hunt's shot is deflected wide and beyond a young Pat Jennings by Spurs' Mike England. The old floodlight pylon illuminates in the distance

FAR LEFT, TOP: "I'll give you a hand up front." No sympathy from team-mate Ian St John as Hunt nurses an injured arm

FAR LEFT, BOTTOM: Time to relax on the golf course as 'Sir Roger' enjoys a round with Everton's Brian Harris in 1963

Hunt, Roger

ABOVE: Roger Hunt scores one of three at White Hart Lane in March, 1964. Beating Spurs full-back Ron Henry for pace, he finishes past keeper John Hollowbread in a 3-1 win. This Good Friday victory was one of several in the run-in that helped the Reds to claim the league title

TOP RIGHT: Sitting it out. On the bench at Anfield in February 1967 with Bob Paisley. The Reds beat Aston Villa 1-0 thanks to a Gordon Milne strike

LEFT: Hunt is ready to take advantage of any goalkeeping slip-up, at Leyton Orient's Brisbane Road in May 1963. The home team won 2-1 and there was a good view from the terraced houses

Hyypia, Sami

A modern day colossus. Sami plays on 'Terry Butcher-style' after a head wound and slides in front of the Anfield Road end (left) after scoring a superb volley against Juventus in the 2005 Champions League quarter-final

Hyypia, Sami

The emotions of the day got to Sami as he enjoyed his big Finn-ish on his last Anfield appearance against Spurs in 2009. Hyypia couldn't hold back the tears as the Kop showed their respect for him with a giant mosaic

Internationals

ABOVE: Kevin Keegan isn't happy with himself after missing a chance against hosts Spain during the 1982 World Cup finals

TOP LEFT: England captain Emlyn Hughes tries to help Kenny Dalglish see the funny side after Scotland's 1-0 home defeat in 1978

LEFT: Dalglish makes no mistake for Scotland in front of goal

BOTTOM: Roger Hunt in action in the famous 1966 World Cup final 4-2 victory over West Germany after extra-time at Wembley

Johnson, David

LEFT: Liverpool v Real Madrid, 1981 European Cup final. Johnson gets a bit shirty as Liverpool win in Paris

MIDDLE, LEFT: Feet up. Injury keeps Johnson in the dugout towards the end of the 1977-78 season

BELOW: Shooting practice. Johnson plays Space Invaders with his team-mates at Liverpool Airport before flying to Aberdeen for a European game in October 1980

BOTTOM: Johnson celebrates after scoring the winner against his old club Everton at Goodison in April '78

Johnston, Craig

The morning after the night before. Goalscorer 'Skippy' wonders if it's all been a dream in his hotel room after the 1986 FA Cup final win over Everton

Johnston, Craig

LEFT: Johnston keeps his cool with an ice lolly as the Reds head from Liverpool Airport to Swaziland in the summer of '84

BELOW: Life Down Under as the wing wizard of Oz takes a tumble

RIGHT: Craig Johnston follows the ball into the back of the net after scoring for Liverpool in a 1-1 draw with Aston Villa in May '83

Jones, Joey

BELOW: We are the champions. Joey salutes the Liverpool fans with the 1977 league trophy

RIGHT: Joey scores a rare goal against Bristol City in November '76

ABOVE: Joey's all-action style is captured by this forward surge against Bristol City at Anfield in November 1977 but his header went over the bar during a 1-1 draw

RIGHT: Joey runs the gamut of emotions before and after the 1977 FA Cup final against Manchester United

Keegan, Kevin

FROM THE TOP: The referee gets a perfect view while Trevor Francis and Bob Latchford look on in anguish but Keegan just failed to complete a hat-trick with this header in the 3-2 defeat of Birmingham City in January 1974

This celebration at Old Trafford proved a little premature as Leicester City's Graham Cross clears KK's header off the line during the FA Cup semi-final stalemate in March 1974

An exuberant celebration as Kevin throws the ball into the Kop following Steve Heighway's winner against Leeds in 1974

The Reds were held to a goalless draw by Sheffield United when the two sides met at Anfield in March 1975. This Keegan effort came as close as any to breaking the deadlock, going inches wide

Keegan, Kevin

ABOVE: How's that for wall control? Keegan practises his skills after training at Melwood

FROM TOP, LEFT TO RIGHT: Super Kev obliges for the autograph hunters towards the end of his Liverpool career in April 1977

Apples 'n' pairs of trousers worn too high. Keegan leaves a plane at Liverpool

Airport following one of our European adventures

With hair like that Mighty Mouse obviously ate the crusts on his bread when he was young and, judging by this picture, he was hungry for success during his days with SV Hamburg(er)

It's like a scene from the 'Last Supper' as Liverpool players make light of the power

saving programme introduced by the club in December 1973

Kev shares in the joy of supporters following the Reds' 1974 FA Cup success

"I say Tosh, I'd love it if we stopped United from winning the title!" A 0-0 draw at Old Trafford in February 1976 helped Keegan and the boys do just that as they went on to be crowned champions

Kennedy, Alan

TOP: Ian Rush looks like he still can't believe 'Barney Rubble' scored the penalty shoot-out winner as they celebrate beating Roma in Rome in 1984

ABOVE: Who would have thought Kennedy would be the match-winner against Real Madrid in Paris in 1981? Here he is scoring the goal that won the European Cup for the Reds

RIGHT: Kennedy takes a dip in a swimming pool at a farmhouse in Rainford. It's a long story!

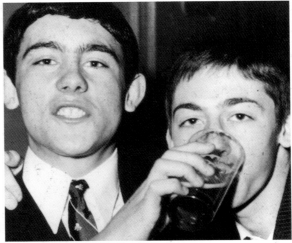

Kennedy, Ray

ABOVE: A young Ray Kennedy enjoys a drink with Charlie George during his Arsenal days in the Sixties

LEFT: We did it babe! Ray Kennedy pictured at home with his daughter Cora the morning after scoring in Liverpool's 3-0 semi-final win over Borussia Moenchengladbach in the '78 European Cup

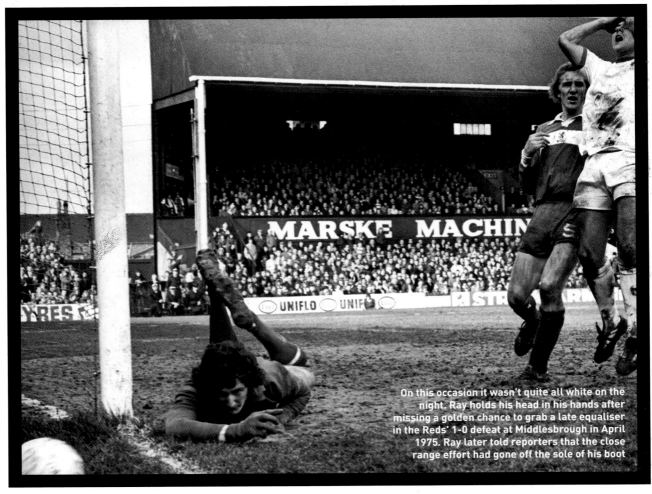

On this occasion it wasn't quite all white on the night. Ray holds his head in his hands after missing a golden chance to grab a late equaliser in the Reds' 1-0 defeat at Middlesbrough in April 1975. Ray later told reporters that the close range effort had gone off the sole of his boot

Kennedy, Ray

Another typical break from midfield by Kennedy during the Merseyside derby at Anfield in October 1979. He is shown beating Mark Higgins to the ball prior to putting the Reds 2-1 up. The game finished in a 2-2 draw and will best be remembered for the 20-man brawl which led to Terry McDermott and Garry Stanley receiving their marching orders

Kennedy, Ray

ABOVE: Kennedy wheels away after beating goalkeeper Colin Boulton to net the Reds' first goal in the 2-2 draw with Derby County in December 1974

RIGHT: Ray of sunshine. Sharing a joke with Terry Mac in training

BELOW: The player who Bob Paisley had more transfer enquiries about than any other signs autographs at Melwood

Kop, The

LEFT: Otherwise known as Anfield's 'twelfth man'. The most famous football stand in the world. Some say the Kop lost part of its soul when it was changed to all-seater after the 1993-1994 season, but anyone who was there on the night Liverpool beat Chelsea 1-0 in the Champions League semi-final in 2005, including the opposition players, will tell you otherwise. Even those who witnessed the great nights against Inter Milan and St Etienne admit that the wall of noise and full-blooded passion that night has probably never been bettered

BELOW: The Messiah meets his people. Shanks and the Kop in its heyday

Lawler, Chris

TOP: The full-back who scored more goals than a lot of midfielders slips the winner past the intimidating sideburns of the Southampton keeper in an FA Cup tie in February 1971

LEFT: Soaking up the Anfield atmosphere. The 'Quiet Man' Lawler trudges off as the first leg of the UEFA Cup final against Moenchengladbach is rained off after 28 minutes

BELOW: Lawler, who always liked to support the attack, tries his luck in front of goal with a spectacular scissors kick

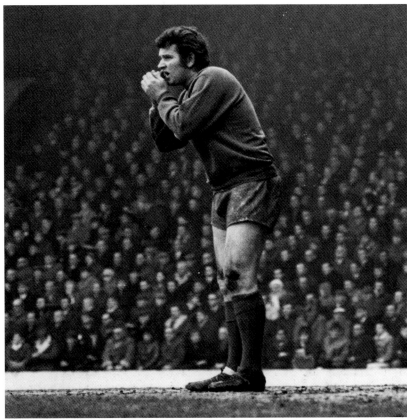

Lawrence, Tommy

ABOVE: Who needs gloves when you've got hands like this?

LEFT: A bit of central heating for the hands in an icy January clash with West Brom in 1970

Lawrence, Tommy

FROM THE TOP: The 'Flying Pig' at his brilliant best. Tommy dives to intercept a shot from Wolves' Hugh McIllmoyle during a 2-1 win at Anfield in February 1965

Lawrence rushes out to save smartly at the feet of Sheffield Wednesday's Tony Ford during September 1966. The game ended in a 1-1 draw

Not even a World Cup hero could outdo an in-form Tommy as he keeps his eye on the ball to save in spectacular style from Geoff Hurst as a Peter Thompson brace gave the Reds a 2-0 win over West Ham at Anfield in January 1967

Lawrenson, Mark

ABOVE: Today, Mark Lawrenson earns his corn as a pundit by keeping a close eye on the action. Here, he watches closely as he nets the Reds' sixth goal in a 7-0 European Cup win over Oulu Palloseura at Anfield in September 1981

Lee, Sammy

LEFT: A fam-Lee affair. Sammy's mum gives the 18-year-old a good luck hug before a game. And watching and learning (below), a young Sammy sits in the Anfield dugout in March, 1977, hoping to follow in the footsteps of his Anfield idols

Singing in the reign. Sammy enjoys the moment as the Reds celebrate the 1981 European Cup final win over Real Madrid

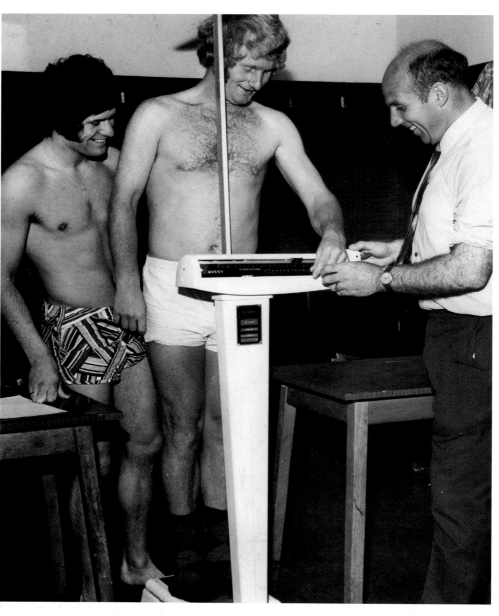

Lindsay, Alec

RIGHT: The one that got away. Many Kopites will remember this left foot screamer from the boot of Lindsay in the FA Cup final of 1974. Future Anfield left-back Alan Kennedy can only look on as Lindsay's shot finds the net. Sadly, Lindsay's moment of fame was cut short when the referee ruled the goal out

ABOVE: Weight your turn. Phil Boersma is next in line behind Lindsay as trainer Ronnie Moran monitors the scales in 1972

Liddell, Billy

The legendary Scottish forward is still regarded by many older fans as Liverpool's greatest player of all time. He had a fierce shot and the speed of a gazelle. Here he is practising his famous headers at Anfield

Liddell, Billy

FROM THE TOP: Not this time. Liddell looks on as his effort at Bristol Rovers goes just wide in April 1956. But the Reds won 2-1 with Billy scoring 28 goals in 39 league games as the team finished third in Division Two

A Liddell header causes panic in the Lincoln defence during a Division Two fixture at Sincil Bank

Billy leaves the Barnsley keeper floored during the Reds' 2-1 win over the Tykes in March 1957

ABOVE: Liddell-pool in action. Well, Billy enjoying a relaxing game of billiards with some of his team-mates in March 1949

McAllister, Gary

RIGHT: Call me the King, or Alaves Presley. Hamann is all shook up with Macca after the golden own goal that clinched the UEFA Cup and the treble in Dortmund

ABOVE: Getting carried away. Gary Mac is swept away on a tide of emotion after his final game for the Reds. His departure, after such an impact, left Reds fans wishing they had seen him in a red shirt long before he came on a free transfer from Coventry as a highly experienced 35-year-old

McDermott, Terry

McDermott's passing and off-the-ball running were second to none, but he'll also be remembered for his habit of bursting forward and scoring breathtaking goals. Here he is celebrating in typical style at Anfield

McDermott, Terry
Everton are in limbo and so is McDermott with his elastic celebration
after Tosh had made it three in a 3-1 derby victory in October 1976

McDermott, Terry

TOP: Terry Mac heads towards goal against Everton, but who's that on the roof of the Annie Road? The fan's identity remains a mystery to this day but he had one of the best spots in the house to see John Toshack knock in the rebound to make it 3-1 to the Reds

ABOVE: Terry realises he's been playing for the wrong side after swapping his Magpies shirt with a member of the victorious Liverpool team in the 1974 FA Cup final. It felt so good he wore it again . . . and again . . . and again . . .

LEFT: Aye, aye captain! Terry isn't happy with Thommo's baggage allowance as Phil Neal looks on

BELOW: Kirkby's finest, Terry McDermott and Phil Thompson discussing a night out in The Falcon, perhaps...

BOTTOM: 'We're cone-a win the cup'. Terry McDermott sums up the relaxed mood in the camp ahead of the European Cup final against Borussia Moenchengladbach in Rome, 1977

McMahon, Steve

RIGHT: The drinks are on you Steve, as Aldo and Beardo celebrate landing the title at home to Tottenham with four games to spare in 1987-88

BELOW: Midfield powerhouse McMahon could hit a ball from distance but this free-kick went over the bar against his old club Everton

McManaman, Steve

FROM LEFT TO RIGHT:
The Wembley hero scores in the 1995 Coca Cola Cup final

Hat's so funny. Macca shares a joke with his mate Robbie on a trip to Spain to face Celta Vigo in the UEFA Cup in 1998

Jason McAteer tries to get a good look at the message on McManaman's t-shirt after he'd scored against Spurs in 1996

Milne, Gordon

Gordon Milne can't believe it as he steers his close range shot into the side-netting during this 2-1 win over Chelsea at Anfield in December 1966

Molby, Jan

Get in you beauty! Molby scores a cracker against York City in the FA Cup fifth round replay in February 1986

RIGHT: Molby leaps for joy after scoring Liverpool's first in the 2-1 win over Sheffield Wednesday on Boxing Day 1989

TOP RIGHT: Calmly does it. Molby scores against Watford in the FA Cup sixth round replay to secure a semi-final place against Southampton in 1986

Moran, Ronnie

**Hard as nails. Ronnie Moran's head almost
bursts the ball as he stops a shot on the line
against Blackburn at Ewood Park in 1962**

Neal, Phil

ABOVE: The Heighway man and his accomplice Neal get away with the silver at Wembley in 1978, stealing Kenny's earlier trick of jumping over the hoardings along the way

TOP: On the run. Marauding down the right flank at Highbury in a goalless draw from November 1979

RIGHT: It takes three to lift the 1978 European Cup

N

Neal, Phil

ABOVE: This is your captain speaking. Neal takes control of the cockpit on a flight into Europe

RIGHT: Driving force. Skipper Neal boards the coach to Vienna for a third round European Cup game in 1985

FAR RIGHT, TOP: Penalty king Neal is spot on against Everton in a 3-1 win at Anfield in October 1976

FAR RIGHT, BOTTOM: Tommy Caton just gets the better of Neal as he launches another attack in the Reds' 2-0 league win against Manchester City in March 1980

A great signing. October, 1981, and smiles for the cameras as Nicol arrives at Anfield

Nicol, Steve

Up and over. Steve beats Eric Young but can't keep his header down in this picture from a League Cup clash against Brighton in October 1985

FAR LEFT: Rush scored one . . . and so did Stevie Nicol. The Blues are down and out as the two Reds heroes celebrate their third goal in a 3-0 derby win over Everton at Anfield in November 1983. Michael Robinson got the second

Own Goals

Watching and hoping...Gary McAllister, Steven Gerrard, Markus Babbel and Dietmar Hamann look on hopefully as Delfi Geli of Alaves flicks a header past his own keeper for the deciding goal in the 2001 UEFA Cup final and (bottom) Djimi Traore provides what fans of other clubs could call a comedy own goal as the Reds were knocked out of the FA Cup in 2005

Owen, Michael

RIGHT: Owen lifts the FA Cup, some would say single-handedly, after his amazing late double against Arsenal in 2001

BELOW: 1-0 down, 2-1 up, Michael Owen won the Cup . . . the magic of Cardiff, and Owen as he scores the winner

Paisley, Bob

TOP: A canny genius at work in the dugout

MIDDLE: Paisley and the 'old lady'. He lifted the Football League championship trophy six times during nine seasons as manager

BOTTOM: That's my boys! Bob leads the pride of Merseyside out at Anfield

FAR RIGHT: A wide smile from the boss and a ruffle of Smithy's hair after Everton have been beaten in the 1977 FA Cup semi-final replay

Paisley, Bob

A lap of honour at the end of Paisley's first season as manager

Paisley, Bob

RIGHT: Back to my roots. Paisley has a special 'cuppa' with his old mates in his home village, Hetton le Hole, in the north east

FAR RIGHT: Do you need a ticket for one of these? Bob brings the European Cup home for the second time in 1978

MIDDLE: From Bells Manager of the Month (a record 16 times by the time he was pictured here in January 1982) to wedding bells as Bob's daughter Christine ties the knot. The wedding was postponed until the football season was over, to allow for Liverpool's UEFA Cup and league Double victory parade in 1976

BOTTOM: Testing a striker's reactions. Paisley flings Ian St John his plane ticket for a flight to Portugal where Liverpool would play Vitoria Setubal in the Fairs Cup

Paisley, Bob

TOP: Another day. Another trophy. All part of a quiet day's work for the most successful manager in Liverpool's history

ABOVE: Keeping an eye on the lads at Melwood

RIGHT: He looks like a normal granddad in his armchair. He was softly spoken in public, but Paisley didn't conquer Europe with Liverpool by being a soft touch

Quickest hat-trick

It took Robbie Fowler just four minutes and 33 seconds to score a hat-trick against Arsenal on August 28, 1994. Here he is pictured celebrating his third – a record for the quickest treble in both Liverpool and Premier League history

Reds on tour

LEFT: Players, officials and other halves about to set off for the annual staff trip to Blackpool in July 1950. Everyone appears well wrapped up for a day in the height of summer

TOP, FROM LEFT: The Reds fly off to Dublin for pre-season in the summer of 1979. Terry Mac's perm already looks as though it has been caught in a jet stream

About to board a plane to Belfast in July 1968 at the old Speke airport. On the extreme left is Tommy Lawrence who, on this occasion, really was 'the flying pig'

Bound for Germany and a UEFA Cup tie with Eintracht Frankfurt in September 1972. Lots of sideburns in evidence

Reds on tour

RIGHT: The Liverpool players enjoy a refreshing drink after training while on tour on a hot Belgrade day in 1936

TOP: Skins v skins. A practice match from the same trip to Belgrade

Riise, John Arne

Hey Arne Riise...ooh...ah...we wanna know-oh-oh how you scored that goal! Another left-footed rocket is celebrated in six-pack style in the days before yellow cards were introduced for taking your shirt off

Rosenthal, Ronny

With seven goals in the final seven games of the 1989/90 season, rocket Ronny played a huge part in Liverpool winning title number 18. He was rewarded for his efforts with this nice piece of silverware

Reina, Pepe

The super Spaniard proves he's one of Melwood's top characters by turning a cone and a ball into an ice cream

LEFT: Pepe shows his atleticism and ball-juggling skills against Manchester City in November 2009

RIGHT: Reina finds thousands of people standing behind him who are just as happy as he is with a second goal against Spurs in 2010

Rush, Ian

All you need is Rush. The master marksman focusing on his goals in the dressing room and boy did he score some. With 346 in all competitions, he is the most prolific striker in Liverpool's history

Rush, Ian

Three FA Cup finals at Wembley, five goals.
Rushie still holds the record for the number of
goals scored in FA Cup finals and also scored
more goals at Wembley than any other
non-Englishman. Here are three of the goals -
his equaliser against Everton in 1986 (top), his
winner against the Blues in 1989 (middle) and
(bottom) this clincher against Sunderland
in 1992

FAR RIGHT, TOP: Plenty in reserve. But hardly
anyone watching as Rushie makes a comeback
from injury at Anfield

FAR RIGHT, BOTTOM: Rushie wheels away in
familiar celebratory style as he scores one of
his two goals in Liverpool's superb 2-1
European Cup semi-final win at Dinamo
Bucharest in 1984

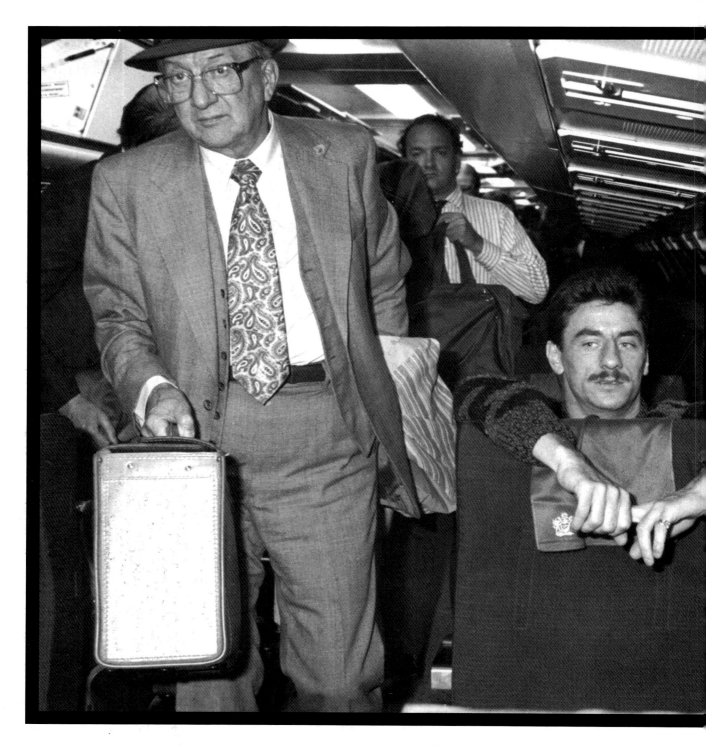

Rush, Ian

**First class player, economy class seating.
Rushie takes the plane over to Italy to sign for
Juventus in 1987**

ABOVE: Classic kit, famous European night. Rushie celebrates scoring the crucial winner in Bilbao in November 1983

TOP: Rush takes a final salute from the Kop in April 1996

It's the first day of pre-season training in July 1970 and Shanks has already got his players flat-out at Melwood

Shankly, Bill

TOP: Wrapped up against the icy Melwood elements for a spot of goalkeeping practice and getting in a bit of target practice (left)

ABOVE: With the card presented to him by the Kop after his retirement

RIGHT: Surveying his kingdom from the outside. Shanks in an early photograph on the approach steps to the back entrance of the Kop

TOP RIGHT: Sort it out boys. Shanks comes down from the directors box to make some changes after Arsenal had scored a second goal at Anfield in February 1973

Shankly, Bill

TOP: Adoration from the Anfield faithful during a pre-match walkabout

ABOVE: The prayers are answered as Shankly's men are crowned champions again in 1972-73

LEFT: Shankly had the power to make grown, bearded men cry, especially here at his last match before retirement. It was the first Charity Shield game to be played at Wembly and the last time Shankly would lead the Reds out in August 1974. A 1-1 draw with Leeds saw Liverpool prosper 6-5 on penalties and saw Shanks go out as a winner. Of course.

LEFT: Shankly on the bench with Ronnie Moran, Bob Paisley and Reuben Bennett. It was the night Liverpool landed their first European trophy, after holding on for a 3-2 aggregate win over Borussia Moenchengladbach in 1973

BELOW: The classic pose. A hero worshipped by his people

Shankly, Bill

ABOVE: Thinking tactics at the training ground

LEFT: Learning from the master. Even Brian Clough would keep quiet when Shankly was speaking. This was Bill's final official game as Liverpool manager - the 1974 Charity Shield

BELOW: "Can we have our ball back, Mister?" There is no-one to hear Shankly's plea

RIGHT: A man alone with his thoughts. A contemplative Shankly before the 1974 FA Cup final. Perhaps he knew the end was near

Smith, Tommy

Big hitters on the steps of St George's Hall in 1973.
Tommy Smith shows off the UEFA Cup, the first European trophy Liverpool had won, and is joined
by local boxer John Conteh who had won the European and Commonwealth titles

RIGHT: The Anfield Iron fists (top) and sharing a joke with Terry McDermott in the Anfield dugout

Smith, Tommy

FROM THE TOP: Head and shoulders above the Germans as Smithy powers home Liverpool's crucial second goal in Rome to keep us on course for our first European Cup in 1977

Smithy thumps the ground in frustration as Pat Jennings celebrates his second penalty save in a 1-1 draw with Spurs at Anfield in 1973

Arriving at London Euston station ahead of the 1971 FA Cup final against Arsenal

A rare sight as Tommy is forced to leave the field with a badly cut head

RIGHT: Tommy goes over the top, this time in a tank

Liverpool didn't bargain for snow when they took an all-white strip to Norwich for this league match in December 1973

How's this for a snowball? And Fairclough gets a game...

You don't get much snow in Spain, so Fernando Torres enjoys the novelty of throwing a snowball

Snow scenes

BELOW: Forget spot the ball, it was more like spot the player as the Reds were forced to play this European Cup game in Helsinki in a snow storm. A 1-0 defeat in October 1982 was overturned by a 5-0 score back at Anfield, on a somewhat clearer night
ABOVE: It was snow joke for these Anfield groundsmen before the days of under-soil heating

Souness, Graeme

ABOVE: Not bad company for the trip home, Graeme. And the girl isn't bad either. Souness celebrates our 1978 European Cup win with Miss World, Mary Stavin

LEFT: Fairclough did well to get out of the way of this pile driver from Souness during the European Cup final against Bruges at Wembley in 1978. It would take a more subtle piece of skill from Kenny Dalglish to break the deadlock

Souness, Graeme

TOP LEFT: Souness the manager cuts into a 'Welcome Back to Europe' cake sneaked on the flight by air hostesses as the Reds return from Finland with a 6-2 aggregate win over Kuusysi Lahti following the club's six-year exile from European competition

ABOVE: Celebrating in Munich in 1981

LEFT: Signing for Bob Paisley

BELOW: Alan Hansen looks on as Souness fires Liverpool ahead against Brighton at Anfield in September 1980

St John, Ian

An Anfield legend whose signing at the opposite end of the pitch to Ron Yeats helped spark Shankly's 1960s revival. Saint scored 118 goals in 425 appearances for the Reds but as well as goals he brought creativity to Liverpool's attack with the boss calling him a "soccer artist". Here he is showing off some of those skills before a game

St John, Ian

BELOW: Is that Craven Cottage or Letsbe Avenue? St John is escorted from the pitch by a policeman after being sent off for punching Fulham's Mark Pearson in February 1966

BOTTOM: Saint salutes Roger Hunt's hat-trick in a 4-1 win over West Brom in January 1968

RIGHT: A looping effort finds the net against West Ham in October 1967

BOTTOM RIGHT: Saint is rooted to the spot as Peter Shilton and a farmer's field keep Leicester in the game at Filbert Street

St John, Ian

From breaking records with the Reds to playing them. Even now Saint is a familiar voice on Radio City commentating on Liverpool games

Strong, Geoff

ABOVE: Jack Charlton of Leeds loses out in a challenge to Liverpool's Mr Versatile

LEFT: Roger Hunt looks dismayed as this sliding effort by Shankly's twelfth man slips under the Southampton keeper, but the wrong side of the post. Strong did eventually score, however, as the Reds won 2-0

Stubbins, Albert

A-L-B...E-R-T, Albert Stubbins is the man for me. The popular Geordie centre-forward is pictured in typical goalscoring form

RIGHT: Following in dad's footsteps. Albert watches his son Eric show off his ball skills in the street and takes a train ride with Eric and his mum before his toddling days in 1948 (above)

Super Cup

Skipper for the night in Steven Gerrard's absence, Jamie Carragher lifts the Super Cup in front of his team-mates after Djibril Cisse's two goals from the bench and a Luis Garcia effort turned around a 1-0 deficit against CSKA Moscow in Monaco in 2005

Thompson, Peter

ABOVE: Despite the despairing dive of the West Brom keeper there's nothing he can do to prevent Peter Thompson finding the target. This was one of 54 goals 'The White Pele', as he was dubbed after a dazzling display for England against Brazil in 1964, scored in 415 games for Liverpool

LEFT: Buying bacon in 1964. He also helped to bring home the title that year

BOTTOM LEFT: England Caps? Check. Neatly folded collection of shirts? Check. Various medals and pieces of silverware? Check. Prototype version of Connect Four? Check. Ludicrously garish wallpaper and shirt that will give everyone a laugh in 35 years time? Check

BOTTOM RIGHT: The birth of a healthy daughter just a day before this picture was taken explains why one-time record signing Peter Thompson can't keep the smile from his face in training

Flying winger Thompson
whips in a corner at Stamford
Bridge in September 1963

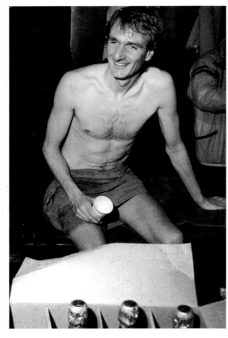

Thompson, Phil

So much for You'll Never Walk Alone!
A young Phil Thompson walks on through
the wind and rain with his home town of
Kirkby providing the backdrop in this
award-winning photograph by
Liverpool Echo chief photographer
Stephen Shakeshaft

ABOVE TOP: That champagne feeling again.
Phil celebrates Liverpool's 1979 title win
at Anfield

ABOVE: Thommo looks slightly the worse for
wear in this photograph as Liverpool celebrate
the second of three consecutive league
successes in May 1983

Thompson, Phil

If there are any researchers for BBC programme Strictly Come Dancing reading this, we've found a nimble footed candidate for the next series. Thommo's flick header found its way to John Toshack waiting just yards behind him but the Welshman failed to capitalise on his team-mate's acrobatic leap

ABOVE LEFT: Hands up if you've won the cup. Phil celebrates the 1974 FA Cup final win over Newcastle back in Liverpool

ABOVE RIGHT: Getting his point across in 1974 in front of Everton's Joe Royle

Torres, Fernando

The super striker has given Reds fans lots of moments to savour since joining the club in 2007 and he hit two as Liverpool beat West Ham 3-2 at Upton Park in 2009

ABOVE: Torres shows he's prepared to get stuck in for his team away at Lille in the 2009/10 Europa League campaign

TOP: Torres gets the Kop bouncing by opening the scoring in a 2-0 win over Manchester United in 2009

Torres, Fernando

ABOVE: Torres seals his first Liverpool Premier League hat-trick with his third against Middlesbrough in February 2008

RIGHT: Liverpool's number nine laps up the adulation of the travelling Reds fans after his goal in a stunning 4-1 win at Old Trafford against Manchester United in 2009

Toshack, John

Big Tosh rises above the West Ham defence to head home in August 1972

BOTTOM LEFT: A grounded Toshack watches open-mouthed as this left footer beats Aldershot's goalkeeper - but the ball crashed back off the crossbar and the danger was cleared

F.STAND

Training

Today's stars could only dream of such a leisurely beginning to pre-season training. This picture shows George Kay's Reds starting their preparations for the 1947/48 season by heading off from Anfield for a five-mile stroll through the streets

Training

ABOVE: No, it's not the Back Entry Diddlers, it's the Liverpool players, including Bob Paisley (left) and Billy Liddell (right), doing a spot of heading practice in the Anfield car park

LEFT: Putting their best foot forward, from left to right; Brian Jackson, Billy Liddell, John Evans, Jimmy Payne, Laurie Hughes, Frank Lock and Geoff Twentyman

FAR LEFT, TOP: The sport is different but the objective is the same as Liverpool's players attempt to get the ball into the net at Anfield

FAR LEFT, BOTTOM: Row, row, row your boat gently down the... Mersey. This picture shows the Reds in a mid-season training camp in Blackpool back in 1955

Training

TOP: All aboard. Tommy Smith seems to be the only one refusing to wear the club issue plimsolls as the players catch the bus from Anfield to Melwood in July 1969

MIDDLE: Warming up for Barcelona. Jimmy Case prepares to blast one in training in April 1976 and Liverpool didn't carry many players in the late '60s but one of the lads hitches a ride

BOTTOM: First day back at training in July 1975

TOP RIGHT: Shankly refuses to blow the whistle until his team have won the Melwood five-a-side, and he's even making Paisley go flat-out for the win and (below) Shanks tells Roger Hunt off for goal-hanging

RIGHT: Brian Hall tries to take on Stevie Heighway on the wing

FAR RIGHT: Woolly jumpers, well woolly hats and warm-up exercises, for Willie Stevenson and Ian St John

Training

The eve of the big one. The players come out of the tunnel at the Ataturk Stadium for one last session the night before the 2005 European Cup final

Training

TOP LEFT: You've been framed! Glen Johnson avoids the obstacles during his first season in training with Liverpool

TOP RIGHT: The whole 2009/10 squad prepare for European action

ABOVE: A team bonding exercise at Melwood in 2004

RIGHT: Cheeky. Peter Crouch slides in to score at the far post

FAR RIGHT: Dirk Kuyt and Jamie Carragher are put through their paces

Kipping Kopite. One fan gets a bit of shut-eye before the 1977 European Cup final in Rome

Travelling Kop

Four times, four times, four times, four times. Jubilant travelling Kopites arrive back at Liverpool Lime Street from Rome after watching our 1984 triumph in the Eternal City

BOTTOM LEFT: Peter O'Donovan was so desperate to go to the 1977 FA Cup final at Wembley that he offered to do £50 worth of work in exchange for a ticket

TOP LEFT: A sea of red and white scarves and flags take over the Stadio Olimpico in May '77

UEFA Cup

**Can someone fill my cup? The Liverpool players enjoy a few celebratory drinks
with their wives in the away club's lounge after winning the UEFA Cup in Borussia
Moenchengladbach in May 1973**

UEFA Cup

ABOVE: Anfield Iron Tommy Smith sizes up Dynamo Dresden's giant skipper in the UEFA Cup quarter-final second leg in Germany. The Reds won 1-0 on the night, making it 3-0 on aggregate

LEFT: It's ours boys! Shanks has a moment alone in the Borussia dressing room after getting his hands on the UEFA Cup for the first time in 1973

TOP RIGHT: The tower of Babbel. What a start to the 2001 UEFA Cup final in Dortmund. Markus rises at the far post to head home Gary McAllister's perfectly flighted free-kick in the fourth minute, but the drama was only just beginning as the Reds went on to win 5-4 against Alaves after Geli's golden own goal in extra time

RIGHT: John Toshack gets a shot in against Barcelona at Anfield in '76 and dejected Dutch master Johan Cruyff leaves Anfield with Barcelona, a beaten man (far right)

UEFA Cup

Cup a load of this. The players celebrate the thrilling 5-4 win over Alaves in 2001

Unsung hero

Kevin MacDonald was signed by Joe Fagan from Leicester as a potential replacement for Graeme Souness. He struggled at first but made his mark in the 85-86 Double winning campaign, with skipper Alan Hansen later labelling him "by far and away our most influential player". Sadly he broke a leg the following season and never recaptured his best form

Veterans

ABOVE: Liverpool's greatest veteran of them all is none other than King Kenny Dalglish who was 39 years and 58 days old when he gave himself a run-out as a second-half substitute against Derby on May 1, 1990. By then it would appear that Kenny's brain had gone as he clearly forgot to get undressed before jumping in the bath to celebrate our record 18th league title although perhaps someone should have told Rushie to get IN the bath when he's wearing his birthday suit

LEFT: Cally was 35 years and 300 days old when he brought down the curtain on his amazing Liverpool career in February 1978. He's pictured here in his testimonial year trying an unusual shot from distance at Hillside Golf Club

Walsh, Paul

RIGHT: Walshy can't find a way through and neither can the Reds on Luton's snow-covered plastic pitch in January '87. It was just the beginning of a frustrating FA Cup saga with the Hatters who failed to turn up for the replay while the fans and Liverpool players waited at Anfield in the snow. They eventually won a second replay back on their own (artificial) patch 3-0

BELOW: Walsh celebrates opening the scoring in Liverpool's 2-0 win over Newcastle in January 1987

BOTTOM: Walsh does well to get on the end of this cross but Sheffield Wednesday keeper Martin Hodge denies the striker and the Reds have to settle for a 1-1 draw at Anfield in November 1986

Walters, Mark

Mark Walters enjoys his greatest moment in a Liverpool shirt, scoring the late winner in the epic comeback against Auxerre at Anfield in November 1991

Wark, John

RIGHT: Wark came to Anfield as a replacement for Graeme Souness but it seemed like he was filling Ian Rush's boots as he outscored the star striker, netting 27 times in his first full season. Here he is celebrating another goal

BELOW: Wark waltzes round Coventry keeper Perry Suckling to set Ian Rush up for the first of his four goals in a 5-0 win over the Sky Blues at Anfield in May 1984

Whelan, Ronnie

The Milky Bars are on me. Whelan celebrates
with a Liverpool fan's lucky mascot after
scoring twice to help the Reds lift the Milk Cup
after a 3-1 extra-time victory over Tottenham
at Wembley

Whelan, Ronnie

LEFT: Jumping for joy. Whelan celebrates one of his two goals in the 5-0 thumping of Southampton at Anfield in September 1982. A young Mark Wright looks as though he wishes he was on the other side. Maybe one day son . . .

ABOVE: Ronnie in goalscoring action at Anfield and getting a friendly send off from a couple of air hostesses before the short flight to his beloved Ireland for a European Cup first round encounter with Dundalk in September 1982

Wright, Mark

You beauty! It's a Wright royal occasion as the Liverpool skipper lifts the 1992 FA Cup in front of the Liverpool fans at Wembley

X – sealed with a kiss

Carra shows the fans what it means for a local lad to win a medal of honour in Istanbul

Yeats, Ron

The defensive rock on which Shankly's success was built pops up with a colossal strike against QPR in a 2-0 win at Anfield in September 1968

Yeats, Ron

LEFT: Great Scots. Big Ron with Everton's Alex Young, looking forward to playing a big game for Scotland, or perhaps it was just Hogmanay

BOTTOM LEFT: As well as his formidable strength, the skipper was famous for his aerial dominance as the cornerstone of the Liverpool rearguard. Here he is clearing the lines against Oldham

FAR LEFT: Line dancing. Yeats and Geoff Strong combine to keep the Wolves pack at bay in a 1-0 win at Anfield in April 1969 which saw Roger Hunt reach 300 goals for the club

Younger, Tommy

Signed from Scottish champions Hibernian, Younger's fee of £9,000 was quite a figure for a keeper back in 1956. He gave three years of solid and dependable service for the club. He does well here to tip the ball away for a corner from a Blackburn shot in March 1958

Zany Reds

Alright Aldo sound as a pound.
It's Liverpool's home boys, and they
weren't too bad away either, recording
Craig Johnston's "Anfield Rap"

Zany Reds

ABOVE: "Right, I've packed my Case and I'm off." Smithy larks about with fellow Scouser Jimmy

RIGHT: The ref is keeping his cards close to his chest but John Barnes takes a sneaky look

TOP RIGHT: Cool dudes. Phil Neal, Ian Rush and Mark Lawrenson in relaxed mood before heading off to Rome for the European Cup final in 1984

FAR RIGHT: Steve McMahon gets in the mood for an England international against Saudi Arabia in 1988

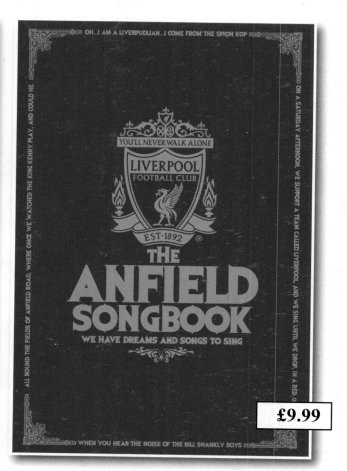